Deep Sea Adventures

A CHAPTER BOOK

BY KIRSTEN HALL

children's press®

A Division of Scholastic Inc.
New York Toronto London Auckland Sydney
Mexico City New Delhi Hong Kong
Danbury, Connecticut

For Dad and Jonathan,
my deep-sea fishing buddies

ACKNOWLEDGMENTS

The author would like to thank the following people for their time and help in making
this book happen: Dr. Clyde Roper, Smithsonian Institution curator and teuthologist;
Dr. Hans Fricke, Professor, Max Planck Institute; Dr. Mark V. Erdmann, North Sulawesi
Regional Advisor, Natural Resources Management Program; and Dr. Deborah S. Kelley,
Professor, School of Oceanography, University of Washington.

Library of Congress Cataloging-in-Publication Data

Hall, Kirsten.
  Deep sea adventures / by Kirsten Hall.
    p. cm. – (True tales)
"A Chapter Book."
Summary: Introduces how scientists explore the oceans to seek or study
such things as the giant squid, wreckage of the *Titanic*, a fossil
Coelacanth, and the lost city of Atlantis.
Includes bibliographical references (p.   ).
  ISBN 0-516-22917-6 (lib. bdg.)   0-516-24604-6 (pbk.)
  1. Underwater exploration–Juvenile literature. [1. Underwater
exploration.] I. Title. II. Series.
  GC65.H32 2003
  551.46'07–dc21
                        2003003913

CONTENTS

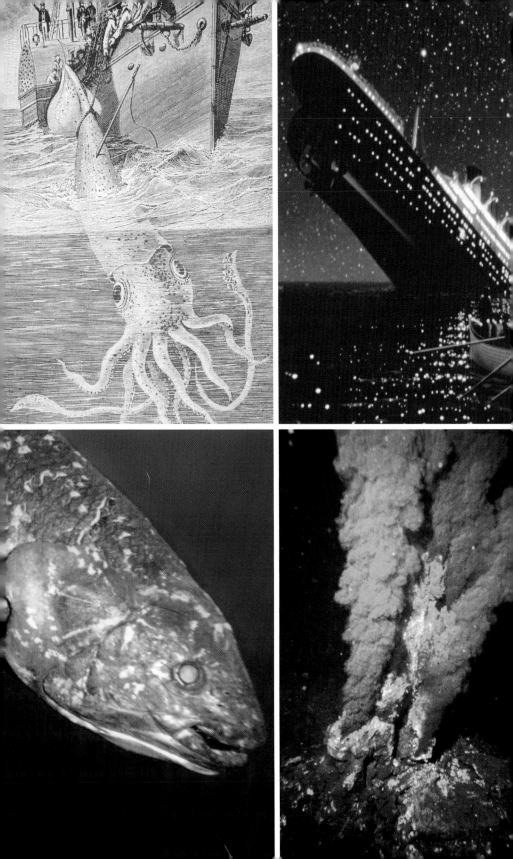

INTRODUCTION

The deep sea is an amazing place. It is filled with all sorts of mysterious creatures, like the viper fish on the cover of this book.

The deep sea stretches from 3,000 feet (914 meters) below the water's surface to the ocean floor. There is no light or oxygen (OK-suh-juhn). Oxygen is what people need in order to breathe and live. This makes the deep sea a difficult place to explore.

Still, many scientists (SYE-uhn-tiss) do explore the deep sea. Clyde Roper rides in a special machine that works underwater. He is searching for a giant animal. Marjorie Courtenay-Latimer wasn't looking for a deep-sea animal, but she found one. Robert Ballard found a ship that had been lost for many years. Deborah Kelley discovered the tallest underwater chimney **structure** ever found.

Read about these scientists and the exciting discoveries they have made.

CHAPTER ONE

LOOKING FOR
THE GIANT SQUID

Not so long ago, people told stories of fights between sea monsters and sailors on ships. They believed that monsters lived in the sea. These huge monsters were supposed to have many long arms.

Today, we know these stories are not true. Sea monsters are not real. Why did people think they were?

Maybe they had seen the **giant squid**, an animal that looks like a sea monster.

The giant squid is an amazing creature. It can grow to be 60 feet (18 meters) long. It can weigh almost a ton. It has eight long arms and two **tentacles** (TEN-tuh-kuhls). The tentacles are even longer than the arms. They can grow to be as long as fire hoses!

Giant squid have eight arms and two tentacles.

On its arms and tentacles are round **suckers** with sharp teeth.

The giant squid eats deep-sea fish and other, smaller, squid. When it is hungry, it shoots out its tentacles. The tentacles grab its **prey** (PRAY). The giant squid's mouth is at the center of its arms. The mouth looks like a parrot's beak. It is very strong. The squid uses its sharp mouth to rip its food into pieces.

In 1861, French sailors spotted a giant squid floating in the Atlantic Ocean. The sailors tried using a rope to pull it onto their ship. The rope cut through the animal and it sank back down into the water.

Since that time, more than one hundred giant squid have been found. Most of them have washed up dead onto shores around the world. A few have been caught in deep-sea

French sailors tried using rope to pull up a giant squid.

Doctor Clyde Roper

fishing nets. Others have been found inside
the bellies of whales.

Doctor Clyde Roper is a scientist who
studies squid. Because giant squid are hard
to find alive, scientists don't know much
about them. Clyde says, "We probably know
more about the dinosaurs than about the
giant squid."

Clyde wants to see a giant squid in its
deep-sea home. He has searched the

Kaikoura Canyon near **New Zealand**.
Giant squid are thought to swim there.
Clyde worked with an underwater
submersible (suhb-MUR-suh-buhl). He
sent it deep into the water two times a day.
Each time the submersible stayed
underwater between four and five hours.

He brought another underwater machine
with him, called an **ROV**. The letters stand
for "**Remotely Operated Vehicle**" (ri-
MOHT-lee OP-uh-rated VEE-uh-kuhl).
Someone can tell an ROV where to go in
the water by using a remote control. The
ROV has powerful lights. The deep sea is
so dark that without bright lights it would
be hard to see anything.

Clyde videotaped
in the deep sea for
many hours.
So far, he has
not found a
giant squid.

DEEP ROVER

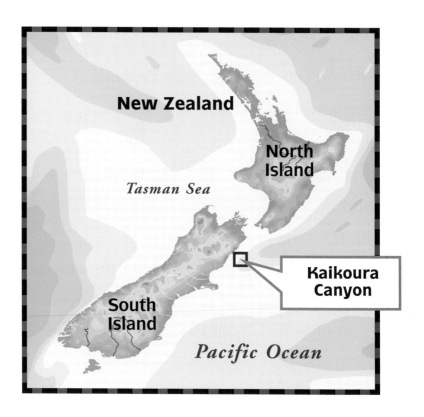

We know what the giant squid looks like. We have ideas about what it eats. We are sure that it lives deep in the sea. Why can't we find one there?

Clyde thinks he knows the reason. The deep sea is so big that there are many parts we have not searched. He is sure it is only a matter of time before a giant squid is found in its deep sea home.

CHAPTER TWO

THE SINKING OF THE TITANIC

In 1912, the ocean liner *Titanic* hit an **iceberg**. Immediately, water began to flood the ship. People headed for the decks, cold and scared. There were not enough lifeboats to save all of the people who needed them.

Out of more than 2,000 **passengers** (PASS-uhn-jurs) and **crew**, only 713 people survived the crash.

Before it crashed, the *Titanic* was headed for America.

A poster telling people about the
first trip of the Titanic

The New York Times.

THE WEATHER.

VOL. LXI...NO. 19,806.   NEW YORK, TUESDAY, APRIL 16, 1912.—TWENTY-FOUR PAGES.   ONE CENT

TITANIC SINKS FOUR HOURS AFTER HITTING ICEBERG; 866 RESCUED BY CARPATHIA, PROBABLY 1250 PERISH; ISMAY SAFE, MRS. ASTOR MAYBE, NOTED NAMES MISSING

Col. Astor and Bride, Isidor Straus and Wife, and Maj. Butt Aboard.

"RULE OF SEA" FOLLOWED

Women and Children Put Over in Lifeboats and Are Supposed to be Safe on Carpathia.

PICKED UP AFTER 8 HOURS

Vincent Astor Calls at White Star Office for News of His Father and Leaves Weeping.

FRANKLIN HOPEFUL ALL DAY

Manager of the Line Insisted Titanic Was Unsinkable Even After She Had Gone Down.

HEAD OF THE LINE ABOARD

J. Bruce Ismay Making First Trip on Gigantic Ship That Was to Surpass All Others.

Biggest Liner Plunges to the Bottom at 2:20 A. M.

RESCUERS THERE TOO LATE

Except to Pick Up the Few Hundreds Who Took to the Lifeboats.

WOMEN AND CHILDREN FIRST

Cunarder Carpathia Rushing to New York with the Survivors.

SEA SEARCH FOR OTHERS

The California Stands By on Chance of Picking Up Other Boats or Rafts.

OLYMPIC SENDS THE NEWS

Only Ship to Flash Wireless Messages to Shore After the Disaster.

The Lost Titanic Being Towed Out of Belfast Harbor.

CAPT. E. J. SMITH,
Commander of the Titanic.

PARTIAL LIST OF THE SAVED.

Includes Bruce Ismay, Mrs. Widener, Mrs. H. B. Harris, and an Incomplete name, suggesting Mrs. Astor's.

CAPE RACE, N. F., Tuesday, April 16.—Following is a partial list of survivors among the first-class passengers of the Titanic, received by the Marconi wireless station this morning from the Carpathia, via the steamship Olympic:

Newspapers gave the names of passengers who were saved and who were missing.

At the time, the *Titanic* was the largest ship ever built. It was taller than a ten-story building and it was longer than three football fields. There was even room on the ship for a swimming pool.

It had taken three years to build the *Titanic.* Those who had made it said it could not sink. They were wrong.

About seventy-five years later, two men went looking for the **wreck** of the *Titanic.* Robert Ballard and Jean-Louis Michel knew they did not have a lot of time. There are only a few months of the year when it is safe to travel the northwest part of the Atlantic Ocean. After six weeks at sea, Robert and Jean-Louis had to turn back. Storms were pushing their ship in different directions.

Robert Ballard

Robert and Jean-Louis looked at underwater pictures on a screen on their ship.

Later that same year, Robert and Jean-Louis tried again. This time they had a new machine with them. It was an underwater sled called Argo. The sled took pictures of the ocean floor. Robert and Jean-Louis looked at these pictures on a screen on their ship. The men had to be careful. If they sailed too fast, Argo might rise too high above the bottom to see anything. If they sailed too slowly, Argo might crash against the ocean floor.

Late one night in September 1985, the men saw something round on Argo's screen. It was part of a big ship. Soon, other parts of the ship showed up on the screen. The crew started cheering. They had found the *Titanic*!

Robert and Jean-Louis had found the *Titanic*!

Since the discovery of the *Titanic*, divers have returned to the wreck many times. They have taken over 6,000 **artifacts** from the ship back onto land.

Some of these artifacts were parts of the ship. They found a bathtub, a door, a statue, and parts of a staircase. Other artifacts belonged to the passengers. There was a marble, a razor and comb, pieces of sheet music, a gold pocket watch, a leather travel bag, money, and jewelry.

A bathtub

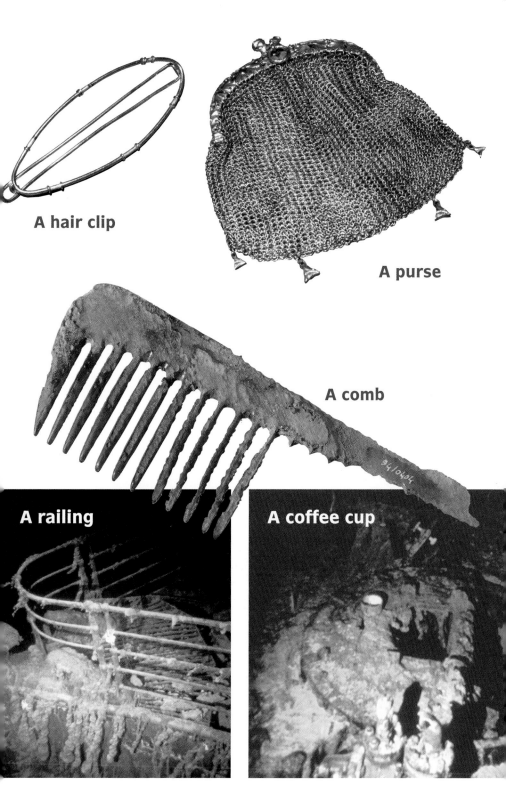

A hair clip

A purse

A comb

A railing

A coffee cup

Some people say the *Titanic* should not be touched. They feel that no one has the right to bring the artifacts back to shore. Other people think we must take as much as possible, while we still can. Parts of the ship are already starting to disappear (diss-uh-pihr).

What do you think?

This picture shows how big an iceberg can be beneath the water.

CHAPTER THREE

KING OF THE SEA

In 1938, Marjorie Courtenay-Latimer found a strange-looking fish. The big fish was covered in blue scales. Its body was hard and bony. It had fins that looked like legs. Marjorie thought the fish was special. She was right. She had found a **coelacanth** (SEE-luh-kanth), a fish that swam in the sea long before dinosaurs walked on Earth.

Marjorie Courtenay-Latimer

Marjorie Courtenay-Latimer said the coelacanth was the most beautiful fish she had ever seen.

Marjorie was a **curator** (KYOO-ray-tur) at a small museum in **South Africa**. She collected fish for the museum. A sea captain had told her about the unusual fish he had pulled out of the sea. Marjorie took a taxi to the docks.

When she saw the fish, she decided to take it back to the museum. The taxi driver refused at first. He did not want the smelly fish in his cab. At the museum, Marjorie had the fish **preserved** (pri-ZURVD).

Doctor J. L. B. Smith

Then, she wrote to Doctor J. L. B. Smith, an **expert** on fish. She told him about her fish and sent him a drawing of it.

When Smith saw the drawing, he knew that Marjorie had made an important discovery. Scientists had thought the coelacanth had disappeared over sixty million years ago.

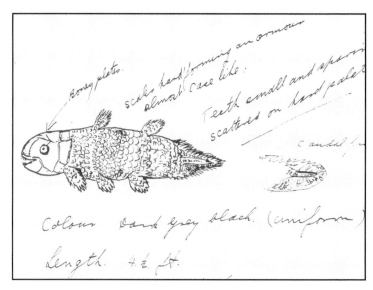

This is the drawing Marjorie sent to Smith.

Since the first coelacanth was found, other scientists have studied this fish. They have learned a lot about it. It grows to be at least 6 feet (180 centimeters) long. Each fish has a special pattern of pink-colored spots on its blue or brown body.

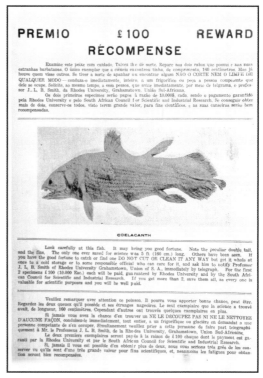

PREMIO   £100   REWARD
RÉCOMPENSE

COELACANTH

J. L. B. Smith offered a reward to anyone who could find another coelacanth.

The coelacanth's skull is divided into two parts. This lets the fish lift and lower its head when it eats and gives the fish a strong bite. The coelacanth eats eels, squid, and skates, a kind of fish. Sometimes it eats octopus.

The coelacanth also eats small sharks and fish that live at the bottom of the sea. When the coelacanth senses its prey, it moves close to it. Using its powerful jaws, it quickly grabs its meal and swallows it.

The coelacanth hunts for food at night. After it has eaten, it swims slowly over the sea floor. During the day, it stays in caves with other coelacanths. It is probably hiding from other animals who want to eat it.

For many years, scientists could only study the dead bodies of coelacanths. What was a live one like? In 1986, Doctor Hans Fricke dived in a submersible off the **Comoros Islands**. He wanted to film a coelacanth in its home in the deep sea.

He searched for many days, but he didn't find any. Some fishermen told Hans to look for the fish at night. On his first night dive, he found one.

Doctor Hans Fricke going into a submersible

Hans filmed the fish. His tape showed the coelacanth moving slowly through the water. Hans even caught a coelacanth doing a headstand for the camera. For two minutes, it kept its head down and turned its body in circles.

For many years, scientists believed that coelacanths lived only in the western waters

A coelacanth did a headstand for the camera.

of the Indian Ocean. Then, in 1998, Doctor Mark Erdmann went on a trip to **Indonesia**. While visiting a fish market there, he saw a strange-looking fish. The people who lived on the island called the fish "king of the sea." Mark wasn't able to buy the fish, but he took its picture.

When he returned home, he talked to an expert on coelacanths. The expert told Mark that he had found the first coelacanth outside of the western Indian Ocean. The fish that he found was a new kind of coelacanth. No one knew anything about it.

Mark wanted to find another coelacanth. He asked fishermen in Indonesia to find one for him. Two fishermen said they had caught coelacanths before. They explained to Mark that they did not like catching the oily fish. They said the fish tasted terrible.

In July 1998, the fishermen brought a coelacanth to Mark. The fish was still alive. Coelacanths can't live long at the surface of the water. They need to be in deep water. Mark put on scuba gear and swam beside the fish. He said it was "a magical experience."

Doctor Mark Erdmann

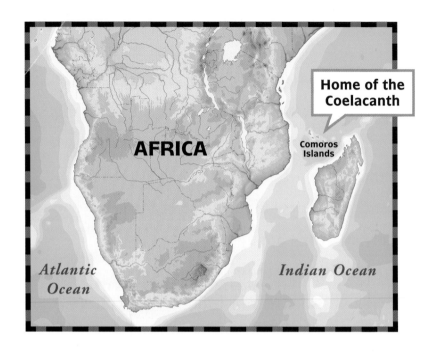

Today, there are very few coelacanths in the deep sea. That number gets smaller very year. It is against the law to catch coelacanths, but people try to catch them, anyway.

The coelacanth has lived for more than 400 million years. If we want this strange and unusual fish to survive, we must protect it.

CHAPTER FOUR

THE LOST CITY

ALVIN, a research submersible, moved slowly across the dark ocean floor. Inside, Doctor Deborah Kelley and two other scientists saw something white shining in the distance. What was it? Deborah and her team moved closer. They discovered more than twenty stone structures. The structures looked like tall towers. They rose up in circles from the ground. One of them was 180 feet (60 meters) tall.

Doctor Deborah Kelley

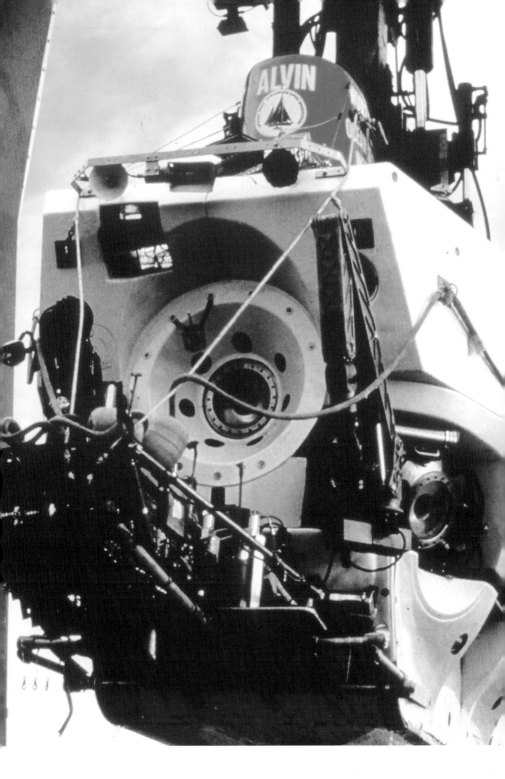

ALVIN is a research submersible.

The towers looked like a gleaming white city
on the floor of the ocean.

Deborah and her team named it Poseidon (puh-SEYE-duhn), after the Greek god of the sea.

Before this discovery, the tallest structure ever found underwater was 130 feet (45 meters) tall. It was called Godzilla. Five years ago, Godzilla cracked in half and fell to the ocean floor.

Deborah was amazed by the towers. "It was clear these were unlike anything we'd ever seen before," she said. The towers looked like a gleaming white "city" on the floor of the ocean. Kelley and her team named the place the Lost City. They named it after the city of Atlantis.

Over 2,000 years ago a Greek man named Plato wrote about a wonderful city called Atlantis. In Plato's story, the city disappeared into the sea one day.

It was never found. It became known as the Lost City of Atlantis.

The stone towers that make up the Lost City are **hydrothermal vents** (HYE-droh-THUR-muhl VENTS). They have warm holes that act like chimneys. Water as hot as 170 degrees Fahrenheit (76 degrees Celsius) flows out from these holes.

Strange sea creatures live around the towers. They live off gases in the warm water. These animals are not very big.

Water as hot as 170 degrees Fahrenheit
(76 degrees Celcius) flows out of the vents.

Most are so small that hundreds of them would fit on the tip of a pin. These tiny creatures are called **bacteria** (bak-TIHR-ee-uh). Billions of them live on and inside the vents. There are so many that it is hard to see the surface of the towers at times. These bacteria are able to live without any oxygen or sunlight. The only things they need are gases to feed on and warmth from the chimneys.

Deborah and other scientists are still studying the towers of the Lost City.

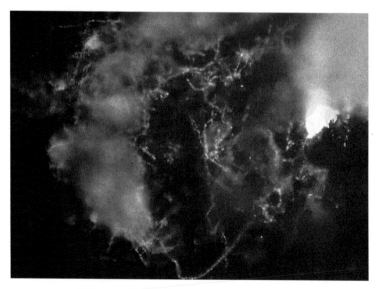

Billions of bacteria can live on and inside the vents.

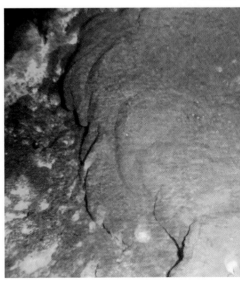

Bacteria live on gases and warmth from the chimneys.

41

"We have a lot to learn about these vents and about the role they play on the planet," Deborah said.

Finding the Lost City has left scientists with questions. Is there other new life in the deep sea that we don't know about? Deborah and other scientists will keep on exploring to find the answer.

GLOSSARY

artifact something that has been made by people

bacteria (bak-TIHR-ee-uh) living things too tiny to see without a microscope

coelacanth (SEE-luh-kanth) a fish that has lived on Earth since before the dinosaurs

Comoros Islands a group of islands off Southeast Africa

crew a group of people who work together

curator (KYOO-ray-tur) the person in charge of a museum

expert someone who knows a lot about something

giant squid a very large squid that lives in the deep sea

hydrothermal vent (HYE-droh-THUR-muhl VENT) a warm or hot spring in the ocean floor through which water shoots out

iceberg a big block of ice floating in the sea

Indian Ocean an ocean that lies between Africa and Australia

Indonesia a country in Southeast Asia

New Zealand a country in the Southwest Pacific

passenger (PASS-uhn-jur) someone who travels in a car, plane, train, or boat

preserve (pri-zurv) to keep something in its original state

prey (PRAY) an animal that is hunted for food

South Africa a country in Africa

structure something that is built

submersible (suhb-MUR-suh-buhl) an underwater machine that is used to study the deep sea

sucker the part on a squid's tentacle that is used to hold on to prey

tentacle (TEN-tuh-kuhl) a long arm of certain sea animals, such as the squid

wreck the remains of something that has been damaged

FIND OUT MORE

Looking for the Giant Squid
http://seawifs.gsfc.nasa.gov/squid.html
How does a giant squid eat? How does it move? Learn more about this amazing animal from the deep sea.

The Sinking of the *Titanic*
www.pbs.org/lostliners
Go on a tour with Robert Ballard, the man who discovered the *Titanic*. Read about the sinking of the *Titanic* and four other ships lost at sea.

The King of the Sea
www.pbs.org/wgbh/nova/fish/anatomy.html
Click the different parts of the coelacanth's body to find out more about this unusual creature.

The Lost City
www.pbs.org/wgbh/nova/abyss/mission/kelley.html
Read an interview with Deborah Kelley, the woman who discovered the Lost City. She tells what it is like to go down to the ocean floor in a submersible.

More Books to Read
Creeps from the Deep by Leighton R. Taylor, Chronicle, 1997

Exploring the Deep, Dark Sea by Gail Gibbons, Little, Brown, 2002

Finding the Titanic by Robert Ballard, Scholastic, 1993

Giant Squid: Mystery of the Deep by Jennifer Dussling, Penguin Putnam, 1999

INDEX

PHOTO CREDITS

MEET THE AUTHOR

Kirsten Hall began writing books for children when she was thirteen years old, and now has over sixty titles in print. Most of her stories are written for children who are just learning to read. She especially loves to write in rhyme.

Since graduating from college in 1996, Hall also taught for several years. She worked with preschoolers, kindergartners, and second graders. Now she works as a children's book editor in her hometown, New York City.

Hall has always been fascinated by the deep sea. As a young girl, she enjoyed deep-sea fishing with her father and brother. Her favorite memory from those trips is catching a fish covered in hair. Even the crew didn't know what it was!